W9-ABT-384

Author:
Fiona Macdonald studied history at
Cambridge University and at the University of
East Anglia. She has taught in schools, adult
education, and college and is the author of
numerous books for children on historical topics.

Artist:
David Antram was born in Brighton in 1958.
He studied at Eastbourne College of Art and then
worked in advertising for 15 years before
becoming a full-time artist. He has illustrated
many children's non-fiction books.

Series Creator:
David Salariya was born in Dundee,
Scotland. He has illustrated a wide range of books
and has created and designed many new series for
publishers both in the U.K. and overseas. In 1989
he established The Salariya Book Company. He
lives in Brighton with his wife, the illustrator
Shirley Willis, and their son Jonathan.

Editor:
Karen Barker Smith

Editorial Assistant:
Stephanie Cole

© The Salariya Book Company Ltd MM
All rights reserved. No part of this book may be reproduced,
stored in a retrieval system or transmitted in any form or
by any means, electronic, mechanical, photocopying,
recording or otherwise, without the written permission
of the copyright owner.

Created, designed, and produced by
The Salariya Book Company Ltd
25 Marlborough Place, Brighton BN1 1UB

ISBN 0-531-14600-6 (Lib. Bdg.)
ISBN 0-531-16203-6 (Pbk.)

Published in America by Franklin Watts
Grolier Publishing Co., Inc.
90 Sherman Turnpike, Danbury, CT 06816

Visit Franklin Watts on the internet
at: http://publishing.grolier.com

A CIP catalog record for this title is
available from the Library of Congress.

Repro by Modern Age.

Printed in Italy.

You Wouldn't Want to Be a Slave in Ancient Greece!

Written by
Fiona Macdonald

Illustrated by
David Antram

Who'd be a slave anywhere?

A Life You'd Rather Not Have

Created and designed by
David Salariya

FRANKLIN WATTS
A Division of Grolier Publishing
NEW YORK • LONDON • HONG KONG • SYDNEY
DANBURY, CONNECTICUT

Contents

Introduction

It is the 5th century B.C. and you live just north of the Black Sea, in a Scythian tribe. Your men are famous for their fighting skills, and your women lead independent lives. Like many rich Scythian people you are a nomad, traveling from place to place. Occasionally, you visit one of the trading ports on the Black Sea coast. There you meet people from many different lands, including sailors from Greek cities around the Mediterranean Sea. They look at you in astonishment. They are not used to seeing women wearing pants or walking freely down the streets. They call you a savage.

The ancient Greeks think that all other peoples are less civilized than themselves. They do not understand foreign customs and traditions. Greek artists and architects have created wonderful buildings, statues, and pottery, and Greek doctors, scientists, and thinkers have made many important discoveries. However, these achievements hide a shocking secret: Ancient Greek society depends on slavery! Without slaves, the Greeks would have no time for art or scholarship. Slaves already make up a quarter of the population in many Greek cities. Although they are surrounded by a brilliant civilization, slaves' lives are often grim. You really wouldn't want to be a slave in ancient Greece!

Captured! Seized by Slave Traders

What You'll Leave Behind:

WIDE OPEN SPACES. Say goodbye to the vast plains and forests of your homeland.

POSSESSIONS. You will have your weapons and your jewelry taken away.

HOME SWEET HOME. This is the last time you'll see your cozy felt tents or wooden huts.

In the trading port, you hear an alarming rumor — Greek slave traders are nearby! The traders trap people themselves and sell them as slaves. They also buy prisoners from warlords who have captured enemies in battle and children from poor families who cannot afford to feed them. You decide to hurry home, but it's too late — you are ambushed and your whole family is captured! Hands bound, you are marched on board a slave ship.

Get a move on!

Up for Grabs!
On Sale in the Slave Market

You have arrived in Athens, the largest and most powerful city in Greece. About 350,000 people live here and in the surrounding countryside; over 100,000 of them are slaves. The trader takes you to the slave market in the *agora* (marketplace). There, you are put on display alongside other men, women, and children. Business is brisk — thousands of slaves can be sold here in a single morning. However, prices are low compared to Greek citizens' wages. A skilled workman can earn at least 1 drachma per day. The cheapest slaves are sold for 70 drachmas, and the most expensive fetch 300 drachmas — good value for a lifetime's work!

Who Else Is on Sale?

ABANDONED BABY GIRLS are looked after by slave dealers until they are old enough to sell.

DEBTORS are sold as slaves by the people they owe money to.

DEFEATED ENEMIES are brought here straight from the battlefield. Some are still badly injured.

Parted Forever!

Where Your Family Goes:
Before   After

YOUR HUSBAND used to train horses. Now he mends the roads.

YOUR SON used to play outdoors. Now he works inside in a potter's workshop.

YOUR DAUGHTER was a quiet, shy girl. Now she's forced to dance and sing to entertain men at drinking parties.

YOU were a respected member of your tribe. Now you're just a miserable household slave.

Becoming a slave means saying goodbye to your family. You will probably never see them again. Your new owner will only be interested in the work you do. Try to forget that you ever had a husband and children — it's tough, but you'll find it easier to cope with your new life that way. You'll feel lonely, but that's normal for a slave, especially a *xenos* (foreigner).

!!!?

Your new owner may give orders for your hair to be cut off — short hair is a sign of slavery. He may also mark your arms and neck with tattoos, or even brand you with a hot iron.

Most slaves are surrounded by people who do not speak their language or share their beliefs. They are not allowed to marry. If a female slave has a love affair and gives birth to a baby, she could be forced to abandon it on a garbage heap, especially if it's a girl.

Handy Hint

Flaunt your talents! Your new owner will treat you better if he thinks you have useful skills.

Put me down!

**!*!

My family! My family!

Back Breaking! Household Chores

Daily Tasks:

Captured women are always needed in ancient Greece, to work as *oiketai* (household slaves). You do all the daily tasks, such as cooking, cleaning, lighting fires, and collecting firewood. You have brushes, mops, and rags to help you, and cold water, sand, and salt to use for cleaning.

SCRUBBING AND SWEEPING take hours each day. Your knees will ache and creak as you crawl across the cold, tiled floor.

STICKY FINGERS. You have to make fresh bread for each evening meal. Don't add too much water — you might never get free from the dough!

KEEP STIRRING! Your owner's family likes oatmeal for breakfast. Try not to burn it or make it lumpy or they won't feed you at all!

Who'd be a slave?

Ho hum...

Back in your own home, you were used to organizing your own time and deciding which tasks to do. But here, you'll be at the beck and call of your owner's wife. She'll give you orders and scold you if she's not happy with your work.

Handy Hint

Try to avoid collecting the heavy loads of firewood — it's the worst job.

***!!* !!**!
Stupid girl!

Personal Services

The ancient Greeks like clean, healthy bodies and admire beauty. But they can't achieve either by themselves. They need slaves to help them bathe, dress, and arrange their hair. As part of your work as a female slave, you may also be asked to massage your owner or his wife with olive oil. It's certainly good for soothing their aches and pains, but it's a very messy task. Female slaves are also expected to provide care 24 hours a day for their owner's children. You have to wash them, feed them, and get up in the night when they cry. You feel exhausted, but no one cares, because you're just a slave.

AARRGHH!

Beauty Duties:

IT TAKES HOURS to arrange an elaborate hairstyle for your owner's wife, and you have to stand the whole time.

You look gorgeous!

DON'T TELL your owner's teenage daughter that she's ugly or vain. It's your job to praise her, however she looks!

BATHTIME IS BLISS for your owner's wife, but hard work for her slaves, who have to carry the huge jars of water.

WAAAHHHH!

Yawn

Handy Hint

Kept awake at night by a screaming baby? Consult a wise woman for an herbal potion to help the baby sleep.

sizzle

Pong

WHICH IS WORSE — your owner's dirty, dusty feet, or your aching back as you bend down to tie his sandals on?

THE LATEST FASHION — scent made with civet, from wild cats! You hate the smell, but have to sprinkle it on your owner's wife.

PALE AND INTERESTING — that's the style for rich women. As a slave, you'll get sunburned carrying the parasol

No Time to Spare!

You will find that slave women have no spare time. When you're not busy with cooking, housework, or child care, you are expected to spin wool thread, weave it into cloth, and sometimes embroider it as well. Each household makes all the cloth it needs for clothes, rugs, cushions, blankets, and wall hangings.

In a Spin? Working with Wool

BOWED DOWN. You may be sent to unload the heavy fleeces that arrive at your owner's house by donkey.

BUZZ, BUZZ! You'll find that sheep's wool is tangled up with twigs, dung, and live insects, which all need to be washed out.

GREEK CLOTHES are made to fit. Check sizes carefully before you start weaving to ensure the finished cloth is the right size.

IF YOU TANGLE the threads or embroider the wrong pattern, you'll have to stay up all night, unpicking your work.

My hair!

Save the grease you remove from the sheep's wool to use as skin cream. It's horribly sticky, but it works.

Handy Hint

slap!

Silly girl!

If your owner has a farm, the wool will come from his flocks. If not, he'll buy it in the city marketplace. If you don't know how to spin or weave, your owner's wife will teach you. Take care with your work! If you make any mistakes, you'll be beaten and will have to start all over again.

17

Fetching and Carrying – City Life

Some Tiring Tasks:

DOING THE LAUNDRY. The Greeks send slaves like you to wash their clothes in streams on the edge of town.

SHOP WORK. If your owner runs a business, you'll have to help in the shop, even if it sells smelly cheese or slimy fish.

COOKING LESSONS. To make stew, chop meat, onions, garlic, and herbs, add water, and boil for hours.

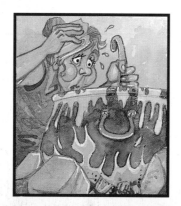

At home, you had horses to carry heavy loads. But here, in the busy city, most of the fetching and carrying is done by slaves. Several times a day your owner's wife sends you into town on errands. She's a respectable citizen's wife, so she stays indoors in the *gunaikeion* (women's quarters). You have to make your way through the crowds along with other shoppers and slaves. You stagger under the weight of pottery jars full of water, huge baskets of shopping, or loads of dripping wet laundry. People jostle you and make rude jokes. You feel as if your arms will drop off from sheer exhaustion. Then you're sent out again!

YOU CARRY goods made by your owner's slaves to the market to sell.

YOU BRING BACK fresh food from the market stalls every day.

Down on the Farm

Athens is surrounded by farmland. The food grown, gathered, and hunted there is essential for the city's survival. Even the smallest farm has at least one slave, and the large farms have dozens. Slaves do all the hard work — preparing the soil, planting and harvesting the crops, and storing them for winter use. They also care for the animals, make olive oil, wine, and cheese, and gather wild foods. The Greek countryside is beautiful but harsh. The land is hilly, stony, and prone to earthquakes, and there are snakes, wolves, and bears. It's very hot in summer, but windy and wet in winter.

Hee haw!

!!**! !!**

The Farming Year

LATE SPRING. You help with haymaking — drying grass for the animals' food.

SUMMER. You winnow the wheat and barley, separating the grain from the chaff.

LATE SUMMER. You use sticks to beat the olive trees so that the fruit falls to the ground.

WHEN THE OLIVES have been crushed to make oil, you pour it into jars.

AUTUMN. You go to the forests to gather berries, nuts, and mushrooms.

Handy Hint

Don't walk in the fields alone. You might be kidnapped by other farmers on the lookout for extra slaves.

 oooWWWww!

Chomp!

Slurp!

WINTER. You look at the cheeses made earlier in the year. Are they maturing or full of maggots?

EARLY SPRING. You look after the newborn animals. They're always hungry!

JUST IGNORE the rude remarks of the male farmworkers and slaves. They're a rough bunch! But their lives are hard, too. They have to work outside in all kinds of weather, plowing, sowing seeds, harvesting crops, and tending sheep and goats on the wild mountainsides.

Lucky You! A Good Home

The Best You Can Get

You might be lucky and be purchased by a good owner. Some slave owners are kindly by nature. Others find that slaves work better if they are treated well. They give their slaves good food, a comfortable bed, and decent clothes.

A KIND OWNER will treat his slaves like friends. (A bad owner will treat them like animals, or worse.)

DEATHBED FREEDOM. Your owner might set you free as he lies dying. If he doesn't, you'll be inherited by his son.

THE CHANCE TO SAVE. If your owner has trained you in a skill, he might let you keep some of your earnings to buy your freedom.

Soldier

Doctor

Teacher

However, even in the best homes, female slaves like you are not treated equally to men. You cannot do jobs like medicine, teaching, or money changing, or learn crafts such as pottery, building, and stone carving. You will never equal the male slaves who work for the city government as policemen and *dokimastai* (market officials).

Handy Hint

Be nice to your owner's eldest son. When his father dies, he'll become your master.

Banker   *Builder*

Lowest of the Low

> Slaves are possessions that breathe...

PHILOSOPHERS are scholars who study the world around them and discuss the best way to live. This is what they say about slaves (above)!

ALL MALE GREEK CITIZENS have to serve as soldiers. Each man provides his own weapons and armor and a male slave to carry them. Women slaves won't do.

A s a slave, you are one of the lowest-ranking people in Greece. People say that slaves are objects, with no human dignity at all. As a female slave, you are doubly disadvantaged, because the ancient Greeks believe that all women are less important and intelligent than men. They are valued for two things only: their skill at running a household and their ability to produce children. Greek marriages are arranged by families to bring wealth or honor, so the men do not expect to love their wives. For companionship, many husbands turn to female entertainers, called *hetairai*, and female slaves.

Slave Rights!

YOU can't vote, serve on juries, or debate government plans.

YOU can't take time off, rest if you are ill, or leave your workplace.

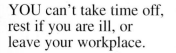

Women are kept out of politics and public life. They do not leave the house except for religious ceremonies, or to run errands if they are slaves.

For male slaves only! Fight bravely if your owner takes you into battle — he might set you free as a reward.

Behave – or You'll Be Punished!

Heed These Warnings:

IF YOU RUN AWAY, you'll be brought back in chains, unless you reach a temple and claim sanctuary from the gods.

Clank!

Smack!

YOU'LL BE BADLY BEATEN if your owner gets angry with you. But few slaves are actually beaten to death. They cost too much to replace.

YOUR OWNER will sell you to whoever offers the best price if he no longer trusts you. You'll have no say in the matter.

TO BREAK your disobedient spirit, you'll be locked up for days in a dark room, with just bread and water.

A ncient Greek law states that men are masters of their own homes and of everyone living there. They have the right to punish their slaves for laziness, rudeness, theft, or telling lies. Disobedience by slaves is an especially serious crime. Like everyone else in the household, it is a slave's duty to be loyal to the man in charge.

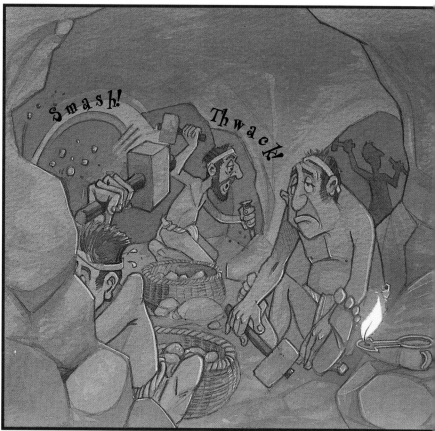

Smash!

Thwack!

Owners are responsible for any crimes their slaves commit. If you do something wrong, your owner will have to pay a fine. But don't think that this means you will get away without punishment! You will be beaten, locked up, or sold. For male slaves, the punishment can be even worse. They could be sent to work in the deep, dark silver mines, where the heat is stifling and the air is full of poisonous fumes.

Keep your clothes on in the mine. They'll make you hot and sweaty, but they'll stop poisonous chemicals from seeping into your skin.

Haul away!

SILVER dug by 40,000 slaves in the mines at Laureion has made Athens the richest city in Greece. The Athenians use it for beautiful coins and to pay for a fleet of fast warships.

27

It's All Over! Your Life Ends

You are old and worried about dying. Like your owners, you believe that a funeral is very important, as it marks the beginning of your new life after death. It should be performed by your family, with all the proper prayers and ceremonies. Unless you are carefully laid to rest, your spirit will not be able to break free but will haunt the graveside or the house where you died.

IN YOUR SCYTHIAN HOMELAND, you would have been buried with your jewelry, mirror, weapons, and sewing tools for use in the afterlife. Here you will die alone and be buried with nothing. How will your spirit survive? As a slave, you've been unhappy in this life. Now it looks as if you will be wretched for all eternity.

How Will You Be Remembered?

IF SLAVES DROP DEAD from exhaustion, they are buried where they fall. As a female slave, you're lucky. You're more likely to die at your owner's home.

A SIMPLE BURIAL is the best most slaves can hope for. You'll be laid to rest in an unmarked grave, with no funeral ceremonies or prayers.

DON'T EXPECT to be mourned after your death! You'll hardly be cold in your grave before your master buys new slaves to replace you.

IF YOU'RE A FAVORITE slave, you may be portrayed on your owner's wife's tombstone. Now people will remember you as well as her.

Glossary

Agora The marketplace — a large open space in the center of ancient Greek cities and towns.

Asia Minor The area of land known today as Turkey.

Barbarian Anyone who was not a Greek. The Greeks believed that all barbarians were uncivilized.

Brand To make a mark on someone's skin with a red-hot iron.

Chaff The dry husks surrounding grains of wheat, oats, and barley.

Civet A strong-smelling substance produced by large, wild cats. Used for making perfumes.

Democracy A system of government where the people of a country have power.

Dokimastai Market officials.

Drachma A common Greek coin. In the late 5th century B.C., it was the average wage for a skilled day's work.

Fleeces The wooly coats cut from sheep.

Gunaikeion The private rooms used by women in Greek homes.

Hetairai Educated, elegant unmarried women who were companions and sometimes advisors to wealthy and powerful men.

Nomad A person who lives a wandering lifestyle, moving from place to place.

Oiketai Household slaves.

Philosophers Scholars who study the world around them and discuss the best way to live. Many ancient Greek philosophers' writings are still read today.

Ransom Money paid to set a captive person free.

Sanctuary A safe place recognized by law, often situated in temples and other holy sites.

Scythians People who lived to the north of the Black Sea, in the land known today as southern Russia and Kazakhstan. Rich, noble Scythians were horse riders and probably nomadic; other Scythians lived in farming villages.

Thrace The area of land known today as Bulgaria and Romania.

Winnow To throw ears of wheat, oats, or barley in the air to separate the grains from the chaff.

Xenos A foreigner.

Index